i

NABROS & Partners LLC First Edition March 2023
For discounts and events:
Special discounts are available on bulk quantity
purchases and for education institutes. An author
event-concert may be requested.

For permission requests, bulk order sales and author
events, please contact:

Publications At
NABROS & PARTNERS LLC. , 4320 Winfield Rd:
Suite 200, Warrenville, IL-60555, USA
i-INVENT.org | Email: hello@nabros.com |
Phone: +1 630 796 7676

Printed and created in the United States of America.
Library of Congress Cataloging-in-Publication Data is
available.

ISBN PRINT –978-1-0881-0987-8
ISBN Ebook -978-1-0881-0995-3

CONTENTS

THANK YOU

*To the family I have
and the strangers I met along the way.
To each good experience
and the bad ones that led me a stray.
To my friends who were there when in
need
and to those who showed me my weak
knees.
To the happy memories
and to the sad ones that made sure I don't
forget.
To the mother of all
and to the father I will meet one day.
I thank all of you for
the adventure of circles and the infinite
moments
in which we finally intersect.*

Dec 7 2014 1.00 pm @1816zenden

ABOUT

Dhi is the essence within one which resonates with …

This resonance of ideas is an effort to compliment one's unique pursuit at work, school and home with Dhi yoga to:

Balance in everything to catch ideas. Open up to all to plant the ideas. Learn the lesson in each experience, be it good or bad, to grow the ideas.A good idea is one that helps us, others and the environment.

If fish are special because they have fins and birds are special because they have wings, you and me, a human's strength is the intellect to manifest ideas.

Oct 16th 2016 6 pm @1816zenden

A LETTER TO YOUR DHI

"As you embark on this journey called life,
remember, you do not have to
become anyone,
you were born a masterpiece,
you are the best and there is no one
else like you.
Taking one opportunity at a time
along the way,
whenever you give your best,
that best in you will be realized,
little by little.
And with each choice made,
you may face a resulting win or loss,
good or bad,
yes or a no…
But, learning to share the lesson in
each experience
irrespective of the result,
will lead you to the best this life has to offer.
Wishing you give the best and learn from
the rest
as you embark on this journey called life."

May 22 2018 2pm @1816zenden

IDEA:

Why do we get the ideas we get?
What are the good ideas?
How to catch, plant and grow the
ideas?

The greatest of ideas come to
each one of us.
What happens to them after
is a mystery.

DHI-001
Oct 18th 2016 7 pm @1816zenden

Is each thing, each one, each
experience just an idea?
Be it a car, house, plane, tree, bird,
fish, country, planet, thought,
feeling, action, reaction, experience
and me, is it all just an idea?

DHI-002
Oct 18th 2016 7 pm @1816zenden

If curiosity is the father of all ideas,
then who is the mother ?

Mind.

DHI-003
Oct 18th 2016 7 pm @1816zenden

What is a good idea?

The idea that helps me, everyone
and the environment.

DHI-004
Oct 18th 2016 7 pm @1816zenden

What does an idea drive?

One's perspective.

DHI-005
Oct 18th 2016 7 pm @1816zenden

What is an idea?

A stimuli for the respective intellect.

DHI-006
Oct 18th 2016 7 pm @1816zenden

What should be the measure
of any idea?

Lessons that contribute to
evolve oneself,
those around us and nature.

DHI-007
Oct 18th 2016 7 pm @1816zenden

With every problem there
comes an idea.

DHI-008
Oct 18th 2016 9 pm @1816zenden

After curiosity plants the idea in
one's mind, give it some heart;
for one will experience it come alive.

DHI-009
Oct 18th 2016 9 pm @1816zenden

If birds have wings and
fish have fins,
what is it that us humans have
which is special?

Our ideas.

DHI-010
Oct 18th 2016 9 pm @1816zenden

Which one is a good idea?

All of them as long as they are used
to help one self,
others and environment.

DHI-011
Oct 18th 2016 9 pm @1816zenden

How do I get good ideas?

Balance time and tasks.
Open the train of thought.
Learn from all results.

DHI-012
Oct 18th 2016 9 pm @1816zenden

How do I plant the idea so it grows?

Share it or write it down some place
that acts as a reminder.

DHI-013
Oct 18th 2016 9 pm @1816zenden

Growing an idea is simple:
talk about it to everyone and your
idea will connect with other ideas.

DHI-014
Oct 18th 2016 10 pm @1816zenden

Ideas are like waves:
They keep coming one after another.

All that one has to do is choose the
wave and surf along.

By the time it hits the shore a new
lesson would be learnt.

Time to go back and ride again.

DHI-015
Oct 19th 2016 11 am @1816zenden

Share ideas that help you, others
and mother earth.

DHI-016
Oct 19th 2016 11 am @1816zenden

They say blood is thicker than water.
So I guess, idea is thicker than blood.

DHI-017
Oct 19th 2016 11 am @1816zenden

When you share your ideas, you connect with others who have similar ideas.

DHI-018
Oct 19th 2016 11 am @1816zenden

Bad Idea: there is no such thing.
As long as the result produced
enabled us to learn something new,
that idea was good.

DHI-019
Oct 19th 2016 11 am @1816zenden

An idea grows when it feeds on new ideas.

DHI-020
Oct 19th 2016 11 am @1816zenden

Is each one of us just an idea that has
been evolving over time?

DHI-021
Oct 19 2016 1 pm @1816zenden

An Idea transforms into a timeless
creation when one becomes aware
of every outcome, gain and fame
that is being contemplated as a
possibility in the manifestation of the
idea; only to set them aside.

DHI-022
Oct 20th 2016 2 pm @1816zenden

Growth of individuals which is physical in nature typically peaks at the age of eighteen.

Similarly one's ideas grow too and reach their peak in eighteen years from the time they were planted.

DHI-023
Oct 20 2016 2 pm @1816zenden

A chain reaction is started by each
and every idea that gets planted.

DHI-024
Oct 20 2016 3 pm @1816zenden

THE IDEA OF DHI:

Balance:
the idea of oneself, "I".

Open:
the idea of everyone and I.

Learning:
the idea of everything and I.

DHI-025
Oct 20th 2016 3 pm @1816zenden

Everyone can copy an idea,
but to grow it one needs to own it.

DHI-026
Oct 21 2016 8.30 am @1816zenden

To resonate with awesome ideas one
needs to practice a balanced lifestyle,
open up to share and accept all plus
keep learning from each experience.

DHI-027
Oct 21 2016 8.30 am @1816zenden

An idea grows when each result is perceived as a lesson to improve for the next.

DHI-028
Oct 21 2016 11.30 am @1816zenden

Time, tasks and expectations are the three key variables that we need to manage as we manifest ideas in the world around us.

DHI-029
Oct 22 2016 12.30 pm @1816zenden

If good results helped one to succeed
by telling what was right then the
logic that bad results helped by
telling what was wrong holds true.

DHI-030
Oct 22 2016 12.30 pm @1816zenden

Is it our purpose to just resonate
with good ideas and bring
them to life?

DHI-031
Oct 22 2016 12.30 pm @1816zenden

Us humans connect finally on ideas
alone.

DHI-032
Oct 22 2016 12.30 pm @1816zenden

It is only time and space
that measure the worth of any idea
and what it grows into.

DHI-033
Oct 22 2016 12.30 pm @1816zenden

If the bees help to cross-pollinate and the fish assist in keeping the water fresh, then what is a human's core function?

DHI-034
Oct 22 2016 12.30 pm @1816zenden

Considering that a human's core strength is having the most advanced intellect, our function may be to innovate and make this world a better place for all species.

DHI-035
Oct 22 2016 12.30 pm @1816zenden

Be like the river
And let your ideas flow
Carrying those who tag along
To the ocean shore
Where Ideas come
To meet their goals.

DHI-036
Oct 22 2016 12.30 pm @1816zenden | Inspired
by Bapu Mama

BALANCE:

How to balance time, space and responsibilities?Balancing one self, others and the world. Balance the mind, heart and soul.

Where do I find balance?

The idea to balance is an opportunity
that presents most frequently in
every thing that we think, feel or do.

DHI-037
Oct 22 2016 12.30 pm @1816zenden

What has balance got to do with
health?

Healthy life style is the art
of resonating with ideas that create
a balance in everything one does:
a little bit of work and a bit of play,
party on and exercise the next day,
rest or relax and being active...

DHI-038
Oct 22 2016 12.30 pm @1816zenden

The cause of imbalance can be solved
when one becomes aware of being
stuck in an undesirable loop of a
recurring idea.

DHI-039
Oct 22 2016 12.30 pm @1816zenden

Emotions vs thoughts or as one says
what we feel vs what we think also is
in constant need of balance.

DHI-040
Oct 23 2016 4.10 pm @1816zenden

Content is the idea of balancing
one's needs.

DHI-041
Oct 23 2016 4.10 pm @1816zenden

Good health is the idea of balancing
one's individual, social and
intellectual needs.

DHI-041
Oct 23 2016 4.10 pm @1816zenden

One can balance only the self
and not others.

But one may loose the balance
because of the imbalance in others.

DHI-043
Oct 23 2016 4.10 pm @1816zenden

There are two contrasting
philosophies at play:

One is focused on purifying an idea
within to the greatest extent while
the other is focused on manifesting
ideas in the quickest fashion.

Balance will finally prevail.

DHI-044
Oct 23 2016 4.10 pm @1816zenden

Past and future balance in the present.

DHI-045
Oct 23 2016 4.10 pm @1816zenden

We all go through feeling
happy n sad,
angry or peace,
love or hate
and so on so forth.
A little bit of everything
is an opportunity to gain a
balance in life.

DHI-046
Oct 23 2016 4.10 pm @1816zenden

Even meditation can kill
when done in extreme:
just like over working,
extensive exercising
or consuming anything in excess.
Any idea exercised in extreme will
cause imbalance and harm.

DHI-047
Oct 23 2016 4.10 pm @1816zenden

Intelligence is the idea of balancing
between common sense,
power and ignorance.

DHI-048
Oct 24 2016 7.00 pm @1816zenden

The equations in nature
are balanced between:
happy and sad,
profit and loss,
give and take,
good and bad,
love and hate,
action and reaction ...

DHI-049
Oct 24 2016 7.00 pm @1816zenden

Working for the heart and soul needs
to be balanced with working
for the dough.

DHI-050
Oct 24 2016 7.00 pm @1816zenden

An idea is balanced in the
dimensions of space,
time and relativity.

DHI-051
Oct 24 2016 7.00 pm @1816zenden

Time is balanced between the ideas
one is resonating with.

DHI-052
Oct 24 2016 7.00 pm @1816zenden

Space is shared with the like minded:
those with similar ideas.

DHI-053
Oct 24 2016 7.00 pm @1816zenden

8 hours for her.
8 hours for me.
8 hours for him.

DHI-054
Oct 24 2016 7.00 pm @1816zenden

Is evolution an effort to fine tune
the balance in the environment and
cosmos?

DHI-055
Oct 24 2016 7.00 pm @1816zenden

A breath is the perfect benchmark
of individual balance.

The inhale consumed is
equal to the exhale produced.

DHI-056
Oct 24 2016 7.00 pm @1816zenden

Watching the sunset on a beach,
one comes to realize
the balance in play between
the sky, sun, air, water and land.

DHI-057
Oct 28 2016 10.00 pm @1816zenden

If there is a balance within then
everything around is in balance too.

DHI-058
Oct 28 2016 10.00 pm @1816zenden

The bi product of balance is health.

DHI-059
Oct 28 2016 10.00 pm @1816zenden

We are built to balance:
one practical while other emotional,
one the father, the other a mother
and so on so forth.
Embracing our strengths be it at
home or at work will enable
mutual growth.
Trying to defy our nature may only
result in an imbalance.

DHI-060
Oct 28 2016 10.00 pm @1816zenden

OPEN:

How to express and accept? Building relationships. Melting the pains, expectations and heart aches.

The idea of opening up is an
opportunity that presents itself in
one's every action, thought and
feelings.

DHI-061
Oct 30 2016 1.00 pm @1816zenden

The bi product of opening up is
relationships and family.

DHI-062
Oct 30 2016 1.00 pm @1816zenden

Opening up to the world around us
in turn opens up the world to us.

DHI-063
Oct 30 2016 1.00 pm @1816zenden

Trust and vulnerability are the two
doors that need to be opened
so as to connect.

DHI-064
Oct 30 2016 1.00 pm @1816zenden

Let not the past experience or the anticipated future get in your way of opening up to the present.

DHI-065
Oct 30 2016 1.00 pm @1816zenden

Needs, be it individual, social or intellectual are born to be expressed and opened up so the opportunity to meet them is created.

DHI-066
Oct 30 2016 1.00 pm @1816zenden

Without an open heart, action, result
or intellect cannot grow nor survive.

DHI-067
Oct 30 2016 1.00 pm @1816zenden

Accepting the immediate result opens one up to the oncoming opportunities.

DHI-068
Nov 2 2016 4.00 pm @1816zenden

Emotions, thoughts and ideas grow
when one opens up and
expresses them.

DHI-069
Nov 2 2016 4.00 pm @1816zenden

An open idea connects one to all
and all to one.

DHI-070
Nov 2 2016 4.00 pm @1816zenden

Train of thought rides on the open
track or open idea per se.

DHI-071
Nov 4 2016 1.00 pm @1816zenden

Fear of vulnerability is the lock that
needs to be opened: mandatory.

DHI-072
Nov 4 2016 1.00 pm @1816zenden

We close down when stuck in the
past or in the fear of future.

DHI-073
Nov 4 2016 1.00 pm @1816zenden

One can open only the self and
not others. But one can close down
because of the others.

DHI-074
Nov 4 2016 1.00 pm @1816zenden

Happiness always hides
behind expectations.

DHI-075
Nov 4 2016 1.00 pm @1816zenden

All kids are born open. Sometimes
the grown up's around them
start instilling their own fears and
expectations in the name of love.

DHI-076
Nov 5 2016 8.00 am @1816zenden

An open individual is the idea of one who expresses and accepts ideas, thoughts and feelings created in each experience.

DHI-077
Nov 5 2016 10.10 am @1816zenden

To open up to others is easy. But to open up to oneself is a challenge.

DHI-078
Nov 5 2016 10.10 am @1816zenden

Each battle that has been fought
over the ages and across the globe
has always been between
love and fear
or between
opening up or closing down.

DHI-079
Nov 5 2016 11.00 am @1816zenden

Each one I meet teaches me something new. Each experience I have always taught me something new.

The lesson was equal to how open I was.

DHI-080
Nov 7 2016 1.00 pm @1816zenden

Practicing opening up and telling the
truth cultivates courage.

DHI-081
Nov 7 2016 1.00 pm @1816zenden

Have you heard the saying
"I was at the wrong place at the
wrong time."

There is a secret to avoid that
from happening:
If one can be here and in the now,
no matter where one is, it will always
be the right place and the
right time.

And then one will experience
opening up to the so called love in
what ever one is doing.

DHI-082
Nov 7 2016 1.00 pm @1816zenden

Said the Pond:
In the past when someone threw a
pebble at me,
I use to think of how to make the
biggest splash and wet that person.
Now, each time I get a pebble,
I look at the beautiful ripples and
wait for me to see my reflection
once all those ripples settle down.

DHI-083
Nov 7 2016 1.00 pm @1816zenden

When words, pictures and books fail
to touch one within, try music.

DHI-084
Nov 7 2016 1.00 pm @1816zenden

LEARN:

Finding the lesson in every result. Understanding, comprehending and realization. Whatever happens happens for my best.

A and F grade are the same if one
learns from each result.

DHI-085
Nov 7 2016 1.00 pm @1816zenden

Did I do my best is the first question
that comes to mind after each result.

Where can I do better for the next
time comes as the follow up.

DHI-086
Nov 7 2016 1.00 pm @1816zenden

Contemplations as in "what if" is the cause of all fears in adopting a fresh idea.

DHI-087
Nov 8 2016 9.00 pm @1816zenden

Profit and loss are the same if one
learns from both.

DHI-088
Nov 8 2016 9.00 pm @1816zenden

In learning to accept and surrender
the personal fears within to the One,
The clouds of a stuck perspective
clear,
Only to be enabled to see and make
the calls of life with a greater clarity.

DHI-089
Nov 10 2016 2.00 pm @1816zenden

"Find your passion" they say as the
talk about success and career comes
up.
But how does one find that?

In doing the best one can and
learning from each subsequent
result, be it good or bad, to do even
better next time,
one finds passion and love in
whatever one does.

DHI-090
Nov 10 2016 2.00 pm @1816zenden

In each experience exist the secret lessons of life. The lesson we choose to learn depends on the idea that we are resonating with at that time.

DHI-091
Nov 10 2016 2.00 pm @1816zenden

The only way to learn is to embrace
the experience.

DHI-092
Nov 12 2016 3.00 pm @1816zenden

To learn to love like a DOG before
thinking of how to be one with GOD
is the core idea of the universe.

DHI-093
Nov 12 2016 3.00 pm @1816zenden

To know that we don't know is the wisest conclusion One may reach.

DHI-094
Nov 12 2016 3.00 pm @1816zenden

After a problem is solved, one realizes the effort put in was just re-focusing one's perspective so as to bring the solution which existed all along into the focus.

DHI-095
Nov 14 2016 12.00 pm @1816zenden

One thing you will never loose:
a lessons learnt,
said Shesha(ava).

DHI-096
Nov 17 2016 11.00 pm @1816zenden by
Shesha(ava) Rajmane (Grand mother)

Anything one does selflessly will
eventually lead one to success and
teach something new in the
due course.

DHI-097
Nov 17 2016 11.00 pm @1816zenden

Infinite number of tunes can be composed from the base 7 chords. So it is not surprising for the science community to observe something new every day in this so called Song of the Universe.

DHI-098
Nov 17 2016 11.00 pm @1816zenden

Typically we focus on the result or what happened first. Then the focus turns to the action - who did what. After which the focus turns to thoughts, feelings and more.

Finally the focus turns to the areas of improvement for next time. Typically this is where we move on or the focus ends.

But if we were to focus one step finer on the idea in each of the steps above, it's amazing to witness one's final conclusion.

DHI-099
Nov 17 2016 11.00 pm @1816zenden

What good is skill if it don't teach
you something new about you.

DHI-100
Nov 19 2016 10.00 pm @1816zenden

To see the unity in diversity is being.

DHI-101
Nov 19 2016 10.00 pm @1816zenden

If each breath is considered
an opportunity,
then the ideas I breath out become
my contribution, I guess.

DHI-102
Nov 22 2016 9.00 am @1816zenden

Aren't we all just a work in progress.

DHI-103
Nov 22 2016 9.00 am @1816zenden

We get dreams when asleep.
We get ideas when awake.

DHI-104
Nov 23 2016 1.00 am @1816zenden

When one takes ownership of the action irrespective of the result, then one discovers responsibility.

DHI-105
Dec 1 2016 9.00 am @1816zenden

I thought it was school and college
that helped me to kick start my life.
But it was later that I realized, it's
actually the life lessons that keep
teaching me.

DHI-106
Dec 1 2016 9.00 am @1816zenden

Perspective plays the lead role in
the act of learning.

DHI-107
Dec 1 2016 9.00 am @1816zenden

Cultivating a habit of exploring new roads; be it to school or to work or to home or maybe on vacation has helped me to embrace new experiences that await me around each new turn in life. And in these new experiences I have found something new to learn.

Ride On, hug that curve and take that turn because what awaits you will only help you in-turn.

DHI-108
Jun 30 2017 9.00 am @1816zenden

Dhi Credits

Everything in this book, be it the ideas, thoughts, concepts, stories, songs, perspectives and knowledge have been written, sung and communicated by many over the past centuries in their own context.

So what is emphasized in this effort is not original in any form or fashion except from the perspective of Dhi Yoga.

Hope we comprehend the words conveyed in their truest essence.

Respect.
Abhi DhiYogi

Oct 16th 2016 6 pm @1816zenden

Ingram Content Group UK Ltd.
Milton Keynes UK
UKHW011825160323
418676UK00004B/299